Advance Praise for
I Wonder...

"In *I Wonder...*, Lisa Goich raises the universal questions that follow a deep loss. She shows how asking is the beginning of healing, and how the comforting answers do come with time. A wonderful, inspiring guidebook for the human struggle with grief."

—Mitch Albom, author of *Finding Chika* and *Tuesdays With Morrie*

"*I Wonder...* by Lisa Goich gifts us 'Good Grief'! No one knows what another is thinking, especially while grieving. An invaluable resource to journal our darkest, deepest, humorous, and most perverse thoughts. Where else would it be okay to tell your well-meaning aunt to 'Go To Hell' when she says your mother is in a better place?! Thank you for this incredible guide Lisa."

—Barbaranne Wylde and Daniella Clarke, Hosts, *The Honest AF Show*

"This book is a great tool for someone who is walking through grief."

—Jill Schock, Death Doula LA

ALSO BY LISA GOICH

14 Days: A Mother, A Daughter, A Two Week Goodbye

I WONDER...

A GUIDED GRIEF JOURNAL

BY LISA GOICH

A SAVIO REPUBLIC BOOK
An Imprint of Post Hill Press
ISBN: 978-1-64293-642-1

I Wonder…
A Guided Grief Journal
© 2021 by Lisa Goich
All Rights Reserved

Post Hill Press
New York • Nashville
posthillpress.com

Published in the United States of America
1 2 3 4 5 6 7 8 9 10

THIS BOOK IS DEDICATED TO:

"I wonder if my first breath was as soul-stirring to my mother as her last breath was to me?"

HOW THIS JOURNAL CAME TO BE...

It was the early morning hours of December 24th, Christmas Eve Day, my favorite day of the year. We all sat vigil keeping watch over my precious mother. My brother, my sister, my dad, and me. We each took shifts while others slept, then traded off, taking turns manning the chair by my mother's bedside. We had no Christmas tree that year—the joy of the season was packed away in closets and the basement, while medical supplies filled the home. We could see the neighboring lights twinkling on the other side of the curtains, flickering on the walls of my parents' family room.

Based on what the hospice nurses had told us, the final moments of my mom's life were near. So we circled her with love and...watched. Watched her breaths, her eyes, her hands, her heartbeat.

My shift started at midnight. I turned on an internet radio station and played my mom Christmas carols through my phone. I set the phone down on her pillow, next to her ear, and ran my hands through her hair singing *Silent Night* and *God Rest Ye Merry Gentlemen*. I talked and she listened. I told her I'd see her again one day and thanked her for being the best mother a child could ever ask for. I told her I would call upon her often after she was gone. And asked her if maybe she could show herself to me regularly through flowers or a song—just so I would know that she was somewhere out there watching. I thought of the decades of Christmas Eves past when she would be tucked away in her bedroom wrapping presents while we slept. She was such a great Christmas present giver. My parents didn't have a lot of money, but what they did have, they managed to stretch far enough to make sure we never went without.

We all watched as the blankets over my mom would rise and fall with each fading breath. One breath. Two breaths. Three breaths. Four breaths. Five breaths…and another breath never followed. My mom's hands that had been cold for days were suddenly filled with warmth. It was as if her spirit just left her body and exited out her fingertips. Floating like a feather being licked by the wind around the room, enveloping those who loved her so much. Her spirit dancing, comforting us, wrapping us up in its beauty, giving us one final hug before retreating to the heavens.

To be there with my mother at this sacred time of her life, was the greatest gift I have ever received. We—her family—were her ushers. Taking her hand and escorting her from this world to the next. Her children. Her husband. Handing her off to her angel guides as her final breath left her body. It was truly a religious experience.

I couldn't help but wonder if my first breath was as soul-stirring to my mother as her last breath was to me.

To get through the painful days that followed, I did what I have always done in times of sadness: I wrote. And wrote. And wrote. And wrote. Transferring my pain from my heart, through my fingers, to the paper. I bought an empty notebook and created exercises for myself to get me past the deep grief.

♡ What's the first step to get through Day 1?

♡ How was I feeling today?

♡ Where did it hurt?

♡ How did this loss compare to others that had come before, and what did I need to do to get through it?

These were all questions I asked of myself to find answers. And these questions are what, ultimately, escorted me to the other side of my pain.

I'm not a therapist or a grief counselor. I'm a griever, just like you. I hope that these exercises I created for myself will serve as an adjunct to traditional therapy and guidance you may need to help you get past the pain you're feeling today.

I urge you to seek help through professionals and friends and others who are close to you who can hold your hand while you heal. And you will heal. It might take a month. It might take a year. For some it takes a lifetime. But there will come a point where the pain isn't as tangible as it is today, and happy memories of the person you lost will begin to fill your heart.

Now take my hand as we turn the page to the first step in your healing process. Follow your own path through this book and make it your own.

It is your story, after all.

With Love,
Lisa

DAY 1

It's like someone turned off a light switch and you're left in the dark. For some it's just a total blur. For others it's debilitating. You want to talk to someone, but you want to be left alone. Alone hurts. Alone leaves you with your own head which is not being very friendly right now. You can't stop the pictures. Did this really happen? You see your loved one, whether it was your mom or dad or sibling or child or dog or cat. Today begins the first day of building your life back to a different version of what it was when they were still in it.

DAY 1

What's your first step? Let your heart guide your pen.

_____

_____

_____

_____

_____

_____

_____

_____

_____

_____

_____

_____

_____

_____

_____

_____

THE FIRST DAY WITHOUT YOU WAS...

(Circle the words that you're feeling)

F*$&%d Up

Horrible

A Shock

Numbing

Messed Up

Awful

Heartbreaking

(Now list some words of your own)

_____

_____

_____

_____

_____

_____

WHERE DOES IT HURT?

Draw arrows or hearts or sticks or stones in and around the illustration below to show where your hurt hurts today. Date it. And come back every so often when your hurt shifts to make a note of it. Use the next few pages to elaborate on these feelings.

TALK TO
SOMEONE

Find someone to confide in. A friend, a sibling,
a co-worker, a teacher—don't bottle up your
grief. Let it out. Your mouth to someone's ear.
Get it out from inside you. Let it flow.

MY GO-TO FRIEND LIST

(a.k.a. People I Can Call When I
Need Someone to Lean On):

♥ _____

♥ _____

♥ _____

♥ _____

♥ _____

♥ _____

♥ _____

WHERE DO YOU PUT YOUR GRIEF?

Are you a cleaner-outer? Or a hide under the coverer? When faced with grief, where does your energy go? Where are you now? Where do you want to be? You just might find that where you put your grief changes with time. Record your thoughts here today. Then come back next week, next month...in six months from now, and see how your grief has shifted.

WHERE DO YOU PUT YOUR GRIEF?

The soul
cleanses itself,
one tear at a time.

THE NEXT TIME YOU'RE IN THE MIDDLE OF A GOOD CRY...

Turn to this page and pour all of your feelings here. Write while you're crying. Circle the tears as they hit the page. Give them a name. Then come back here in a month from now and see if you can remember what prompted those tears in the first place. As your heart heals, you'll find the tears will still have meaning, and you'll always remember their name, but compartmentalizing them will be easier as your soul is cleansed.

A GOOD CRY...

I wonder how
I'm supposed to get
through today?

PUNCH
THIS PAGE!

Punch this page. Right here. Right in the
bullseye. If you're angry, let it all out. Yell.
Scream. Say what's on your mind.

FIND
YOUR TRIBE

Join a grief group online. There are so many
wonderful groups for all different areas of loss.
If you're more of an in-person person, find
a support group in your area that meets
regularly that you'd like to be a part of.
Maybe you have a hobby that you've put
aside for a while; now would be a great time
to pick it up and meet others who share your
interests. Write your tribe ideas here, then dive
in and make some friends. Finding people in
our tribe who understand and who are
going through what we're going through,
is sometimes the greatest medicine of all.

FIND YOUR TRIBE

Everyone becomes
a memory of
somebody sometime.

WHO FILLS YOUR MEMORIES?

Write your favorite memories of people in your life who have passed. How clear are they now? How did you feel when they passed? How do you feel now? How does that reflect the way you process these memories today?

WHO FILLS YOUR MEMORIES?

_____

_____

_____

_____

_____

_____

_____

_____

_____

_____

_____

_____

_____

_____

_____

_____

I WILL NEVER FORGET...

♥ _____

♥ _____

♥ _____

♥ _____

♥ _____

♥ _____

♥ _____

♥ _____

♥ _____

♥ _____

NO TWO LOSSES ARE ALIKE.

How does this loss compare to others? How did you overcome your grief with previous losses? When did you turn a corner? Do you remember the day you started feeling better? Do you remember the transition from bad to good? Do you remember when the sun came out again? Share those experiences here.

LOSSES

I saw you last night
in my dream.
Did you know
it was me?

I'LL SEE YOU IN MY DREAMS

You had a dream about your loved one last night. They were vibrant and alive. You were talking to them as if nothing happened—as if they had been here all along. And it was real. So unbelievably real. These are called "visitation dreams." And those who believe in communications from the afterlife believe that these are actually our loved ones reaching out to us while we are in a state of consciousness that allows them in. Even if you're not one to believe in woo-woo stuff, it's kind of a cool thing to think about, isn't it?

DREAMS

Use this section to record your dreams. Date them. See how they change over time. See how often your loved one stops by to check on you to say hello.

_____

_____

_____

_____

_____

_____

_____

_____

_____

_____

_____

_____

_____

_____

A REMEMBRANCE RITUAL

Light a candle in your loved one's honor every night for a week. And when you do, talk to them. Talk to the spirit world and ask them for protection of your loved one's soul. Let them know you are still here thinking about them. Your loved one will be with you as long as their memory is in your heart.

I wonder if
you're thinking about
me today too?

ISN'T LIFE SOMETHING?

Our feet are planted here in this realm for just a short time. Then one day, this invisible doorway opens, and we're asked to step to the other side. No more communication as this shield to another world closes, and we're on one side and our loved one is on the other. Picture your loved one on the other side of this door. They can hear you but cannot respond.

ISN'T LIFE SOMETHING

What would you say to them right now?

_____

_____

_____

_____

_____

_____

_____

_____

_____

_____

_____

_____

_____

_____

_____

_____

_____

_____

ISN'T LIFE SOMETHING

Now what would you want them to say to you?

_____

_____

_____

_____

_____

_____

_____

_____

_____

_____

_____

_____

_____

_____

_____

_____

You are
allowed to grieve
at your own pace.

IT'S SAID THAT "TIME HEALS ALL WOUNDS."

Nah. Certainly not all. Sure, time lessens pain as memories slip further and further from our grasp. But for some, that process can take three months, for others—a lifetime. Your loss is your loss. And the way you grieve that loss is entirely up to you. Don't let people rush you through it. And never let anyone tell you that "You should be over this by now!" Or conversely, that you're over your grief too soon. You are the keeper of your own clock. Feel free to use this space here to map out your timeline. Come back here to check in now and again. Mark the date. Remember, grief isn't linear. So if you find yourself feeling good one day, then not so good the next, cut yourself some slack.

YOUR OWN PACE

Be like Sinatra—do it your way.

_____

_____

_____

_____

_____

_____

_____

_____

_____

_____

_____

_____

_____

_____

_____

_____

_____

_____

A LOVING SEND-OFF

Your mom's favorite sweater.

Your dad's pipe.

Your dog's collar.

When cleaning out a loved one's posses-
sions after they've gone, save a thing or two
that are most meaningful to you, then take a
photograph of those things you choose not to
keep, and send them off with a loving thank
you and a prayer.

What are some things you've chosen to keep?

What are the things you've let go of?

A LOVING SEND OFF

Share their stories here…

_____

_____

_____

_____

_____

_____

_____

_____

_____

_____

_____

_____

_____

_____

_____

_____

_____

_____

_____

THE "WHAT HAVE I DONE FOR MYSELF TODAY?" CHECKLIST

Check all that apply.

- ♥ I got up.
- ♥ I took a shower.
- ♥ I thought about you.
- ♥ I fed the dog/cat/bird/fish/myself.
- ♥ I called a friend.
- ♥ I washed the dishes in the sink.
- ♥ I went outside and breathed fresh air into my lungs.
- ♥ I made a wish on a star.
- ♥ I paid something forward.
- ♥ I cried.
- ♥ I laughed.

NOW ADD SOME OF YOUR OWN...

- ♥ _____
- ♥ _____
- ♥ _____
- ♥ _____
- ♥ _____
- ♥ _____
- ♥ _____
- ♥ _____
- ♥ _____
- ♥ _____

DRAW A PICTURE OF
HOW YOU FEEL TODAY

I wonder
when I'm going to
feel like me again?

HERE'S TO LIFE!

Go outside and look at all of the LIFE around you. Bring this notebook. List what you see. Document the beauty with photographs. Snap away! Life is everywhere. In a tree, in a flower, in the clouds, in a bug, in a blade of grass. When your grief seems so overwhelming, and so big, take it and place it out into the world and watch life sprout up around it.

HERE'S TO LIFE

LOOK OUTSIDE OF YOURSELF TODAY

Is there someone out there who needs you? Do you know someone who is hurting? What can you do for them that will make them feel better today? Stepping outside of our own selves—even if those steps are baby steps— can do so much good for a broken heart.

(HINT: By helping others, we are helping ourselves!)

LOOK OUTSIDE YOURSELF

Chart your plan of action here.

_____

_____

_____

_____

_____

_____

_____

_____

_____

_____

_____

_____

_____

_____

_____

_____

_____

_____

We only have so
many days.
Use them wisely.

HOW DID YOU USE YOUR DAY TODAY?

What was on your plate today? Did you call a friend? Did you read a book? Did you wander around the mall? Did you eat a pile of French fries while binging your favorite TV show? This is a place to keep track of your daily activities. Logging even the smallest of things will show your progress day by day.

HOW DID YOU USE YOUR DAY?

Date your entries and revisit this section daily for updates!

_____

_____

_____

_____

_____

_____

_____

_____

_____

_____

_____

_____

_____

_____

_____

SOCIAL MEDIA IS FAKE NEWS

People on social media always look so happy.
Just remember that most of that is a facade.
No one is happy 24/7. Few people post their
woes online. If you could be totally honest on
your social media pages today, what would
you post?

WHAT WOULD YOU POST?

NOT SO SOCIAL MEDIA POSTS

When you feel like venting, but don't feel like
airing your grievances for all the world to see,
use the next few pages as your safe space
and post here instead.

NOT SO SOCIAL

WHAT ARE YOU FEELING GUILTY ABOUT TODAY?

Guilt is often a by-product of loss. When we lose someone the "I should haves" and "Why didn't Is?" come pouring out. We always think we could have done more to keep our loved one alive a little longer, to have been a better partner, or to have been a more present friend. But life is life. And there comes a point where you must free yourself from this prison and tell yourself that you:

1. Are human.
2. Did the best you could.

Just remember, guilt is a valid emotion. Face it, learn from it, talk to someone about it, and try to find a way to make sense of it so you can forgive yourself and move forward.

GUILTY

Use the next few pages to untangle these feelings and, while doing so, never forget: you are loved.

_____

_____

_____

_____

_____

_____

_____

_____

_____

_____

_____

_____

_____

_____

_____

_____

I wonder where
you are today?

GRIEF BRIEFS

Small Reminders to Read, Follow, Photograph,
Share, Trace, Color, and Take to Heart While
You're Healing

TALK TO YOUR LOVED
ONE AFTER
THEY'VE GONE.

THEY'RE LISTENING.

LOOK FOR YOUR LOST
LOVED ONE IN THE
BEAUTY AROUND YOU.

THEY'RE THERE.

KEEP VOICEMAIL
MESSAGES TO LISTEN
TO WHEN YOU MISS
HEARING THEIR VOICE.

BUT LISTEN
ONLY WHEN READY.

TRACE YOUR FINGERS
ALONG THE LETTERS OR
CARDS HANDWRITTEN BY
A LOVED ONE.

YOU'LL FEEL THEIR
SOUL IN EVERY STROKE
OF THE PEN.

TURN OFF THE LIGHTS
AND CLOSE YOUR EYES.
BREATHE GENTLY.
HOLD YOUR HANDS OPEN
AT YOUR SIDE.

CAN YOU FEEL YOUR
LOVED ONE NEAR?

SPREAD A BLANKET
OUT ON THE GRASS ON
A SUNNY DAY. LIE ON
YOUR BACK AND LOOK
UP TO THE SKY.

SOMEWHERE, SOMEONE
IS LOOKING DOWN
ON YOU TOO.

WALK.

STRETCH.

MOVE.

RUN.

PLAY YOUR LOVED ONE'S
FAVORITE SONG.

REMEMBER THEM
WITH A SMILE.

SMILE ONCE TODAY.
AND TWICE TOMORROW.
THREE TIMES THE NEXT
DAY. AND FOUR TIMES
THE DAY AFTER THAT.

SOON THE SMILES WILL
COME NATURALLY AND
SPARK YOUR HEART TO
COME ALIVE AGAIN.

BE GENTLE
WITH YOURSELF.

ACKNOWLEDGE
YOUR FEELINGS.

STEP INTO A WARM
SHOWER. CRY AS HARD
AS YOU CAN FOR AS
LONG AS YOU NEED TO...

...LET THE WARMTH OF
THE WATER MIX WITH
YOUR TEARS AND WASH
YOUR SADNESS AWAY.

LAUGH YOUR
ASS OFF.

DON'T FORGET
TO EAT.

WRITE SOME GRIEF BRIEFS OF YOUR OWN

Have you read something that really resonated with you? Need a space to write down advice from friends? Looking for some blank pages to store quotes you've cut out of magazines? Use the next few pages to create your own grief briefs and to record those you've collected along your path to healing.

GRIEF BRIEFS

A PLACE OF CONDOLENCE

Friends have reached out to you with so many kind sentiments since you've experienced your loss. Warm words of sympathy, caring, and shared stories about your loved one lost. Whether they were from cards received, emails, social media, or just thoughtful words over the phone, make this space their home so you can refer to them in your quiet moments of reflection.

CONDOLENCES

BEFORE AND AFTER

What did you learn about your loved one
after their passing that you didn't know
before they died?

BEFORE AND AFTER

THOSE PESKY TRIGGERS

What triggers your memories? What are your
triggers? What triggers you?

- ♥ _____
- ♥ _____
- ♥ _____
- ♥ _____
- ♥ _____
- ♥ _____
- ♥ _____
- ♥ _____
- ♥ _____

I wonder why
I never appreciated
every moment that
we were together?

Here are all the things I never said to you, or asked of you, but should have. All of those opportunities missed. Read my words. They're for you.

Dear _____,

_____

_____

_____

_____

_____

_____

_____

_____

_____

_____

_____

_____

_____

_____

_____

Get a box. Cut up tiny pieces of paper. Write messages to your loved one. Fold them up and put them in your soul box to be heard.

NOW WHAT?

You were here. Now you're gone. Now what?

NOW WHAT?

TEN THINGS I MISS ABOUT YOU

- ♥ _____
- ♥ _____
- ♥ _____
- ♥ _____
- ♥ _____
- ♥ _____
- ♥ _____
- ♥ _____
- ♥ _____
- ♥ _____

IN CASE YOU NEED SPACE FOR TEN MORE

- ♥ _____
- ♥ _____
- ♥ _____
- ♥ _____
- ♥ _____
- ♥ _____
- ♥ _____
- ♥ _____
- ♥ _____
- ♥ _____

Escape into the
world of a good book
or film. Let it take
you away from
the feelings you're
feeling today.

BOOKS
RECOMMENDED
BY FRIENDS

📖 _____

📖 _____

📖 _____

📖 _____

📖 _____

📖 _____

📖 _____

📖 _____

FILMS RECOMMENDED BY FRIENDS

🎥 _____

🎥 _____

🎥 _____

🎥 _____

🎥 _____

🎥 _____

🎥 _____

🎥 _____

🎥 _____

🎥 _____

BINGE WORTHY TV RECOMMENDED BY FRIENDS

I wonder how
long I'm going
to feel this way?

BEFORE I FORGET

As time passes, memories start to fade. Our hearts won't allow them to fade completely, but the details of certain moments, or a person's voice, or a facial expression that you once knew so well, begin to blur. So as to not forget, talk about some of these memories here. What was your favorite day spent with this person? What was your funniest shared moment together? What did their voice sound like? Think about their eyes. Picture them looking at you. How does it make you feel? Write it down here.

BEFORE I FORGET

_____

_____

_____

_____

_____

_____

_____

_____

_____

_____

_____

_____

_____

_____

_____

_____

_____

_____

_____

HERE IT COMES AGAIN

And then one day, just as you think you're healed, something breaks down the door, barges in, and you're right back where you were on Day 1. Is today that day? Write what you're feeling here.

HERE IT COMES

A LETTER TO
YOUR LOVED ONE

Write a letter to your loved one here. Use the
front and back of the next page. When you're
finished, tear out that page and rip it up. Have
a favorite number? Rip it up into that many
pieces. Then bring it out into your garden, or to
a favorite spot that you shared together, dig
a little hole, and place it in the ground. Plant
some seeds in the earth where you placed
it. When life appears in that spot, you'll know
your message was received.

When you're finished, tear out this page and rip it up.

Dear _____,

_____

_____

_____

_____

_____

_____

_____

_____

_____

_____

_____

_____

_____

_____

_____

_____

_____

_____

_____

When life appears
in the spot where
you planted your
letter, you'll know
your message
was received.

REORGANIZE YOUR HEART SPACE

Clean your way to a healed heart—sometimes clearing your environment of clutter can help clear your mind of pain. Start small. One room. Organize. Clean. Rearrange. And while you're doing it, think of the person or being that your heart is aching over. Each step in the organization process will help you reframe the loss. Not forget. Reframe. Change your environment enough so that your world is reflective of your new reality.

Make your healed heart to do list here. Check off items when completed.

♥ _____

♥ _____

♥ _____

♥ _____

♥ _____

♥ _____

♥ _____

♥ _____

♥ _____

♥ _____

♥ _____

♥ _____

IN THEIR HONOR

What would honor your loved one? Plant a
garden. Start a charity. Donate to a cause in
their name that they held dear. Do something
today to carry on their legacy.

IN THEIR HONOR

List some ideas here.

_____

_____

_____

_____

_____

_____

_____

_____

_____

_____

_____

_____

_____

_____

_____

_____

I DID IT!

List five things you surprisingly accomplished this week, despite the fact you felt like doing absolutely nothing.

♥ _____

♥ _____

♥ _____

♥ _____

♥ _____

I wonder if it's
okay for me to
smile today?

THE SEVEN DAYS OF YOU

Enjoying your life will not be dishonoring the person you lost. So shake that guilt that you're feeling and spend this week doing one thing for yourself every day that makes you happy. (That's right, happy! You're allowed to be happy!) Go to dinner with a friend. Buy yourself something you want, but don't need. Get a massage. Treat yourself to a double-scoop ice cream cone! Journal each day on the next seven pages. Write what you did, how you felt, and how it all relates to your healing process. If guilt seeps in (and it might!), write about it. Write how it felt, how you dealt with it, and how you moved on to the next day. At the end of seven days, go back and read through your week. You just might be surprised at the progress you're making! You can do this!

DAY 1

DAY 2

DAY 3

DAY 4

DAY 5

DAY 6

DAY 7

AL{TRUE}ISTIC
LOVE

Abraham Lincoln said, "To ease another's heartache is to forget one's own." Now that you've spent a week practicing self-love, dedicate the next seven days to volunteering your time, love, and energy to others in need. It's been scientifically proven that charity does a mind and body good (and who can argue with science?). Start thinking about who you'd like to serve today. A neighbor in need? An organization? A mentoring program at the school around the corner? What person or group could benefit from your skills and passion? Sketch it all out here in the next few pages and report back at the end of the week.

AL(TRUE)ISTIC LOVE

*Warning: Helping others can be addicting!

It's okay
to feel okay.

SPEND YOUR DAY BETWEEN THE COVERS

Are you ready for an adventure? A place where you can zen-out that's like a charging station for your brain? Head to the bookstore (yes, there are still some of those around!) and just wander for a few hours. Browse through books on grief. Pick up a book on renewal. Look at funny books that might make you laugh. Get a trashy magazine. Buy a blank journal or coloring book. Get some crayons. Take a big, deep breath and inhale the knowledge all around you. Absorb the words. People watch. Fill your head with inspiration. Document your great adventure here!

BOOKSTORE

WHEN I SEE YOU AGAIN, WE WILL...

WE WILL...

_____
_____
_____
_____
_____
_____
_____
_____
_____
_____
_____
_____
_____
_____
_____
_____
_____
_____

NOW TAKE A DEEP BREATH

Ohhhhmmmmm my goodness, this seems like the perfect time to do a little guided meditation, doesn't it? Whether it's through a formal class, an app, or a video online, take a few minutes each day to clear your mind, manage your stress, reframe your outlook, and strengthen your self-awareness.

Ohhhhmmmm

Ask friends for recommendations. Write those recommendations here.

_____

_____

_____

_____

_____

_____

_____

_____

_____

_____

_____

_____

_____

_____

YOUR PERSONAL HEALING PLAYLIST

Music heals the heart. It ignites our memories and takes us back to happy days, summers in the sun, and carefree times when our worlds seemed perfect. What songs would you add to your Healing Playlist? What songs transport you? Make a list here then create a playlist on your favorite streaming platform. Happy listening!

YOUR PLAYLIST

WRITE YOUR OWN BOOK!

Now it's your turn to write your story about life with the loved one you lost. Your memoir. Your life together on paper. Get a pen. Turn the page. Write your heart out! There are blank pages included to post pictures, letters... wherever your adventure takes you!

YOUR ADVENTURE

Don't say, "Goodbye."
Say, "See ya later!"